I0697592

UNLOCKING SUCCESS

ON

FREELANCER

Strategies for Building a Thriving Freelance Career in a Competitive Marketplace.

Table of contents

Chapter One

INTRODUCTION

Starting a freelance career can be a great way to gain freedom, independence, and the chance to turn your talents into a successful business. For independent contractors, the digital age has brought about a new era marked by platforms that link skills to a worldwide market. This book is designed to offer insights, tactics, and useful guidance to manage the ever-changing freelance industry, regardless of whether you're an aspiring freelancer or an experienced expert trying to advance your freelance career.

In the upcoming chapters, we'll explore the nuances of building a solid online presence on freelance sites, perfecting your bidding techniques, refining your profile, and producing outstanding work. Our goal is to provide you with the resources you need to establish a profitable and long-lasting freelancing career, from efficient client communication to fair and reasonable pricing. Come along as we examine the subtleties of freelancing and provide advice on how to succeed in this dynamic environment.

Chapter Two

Understanding the Freelance Landscape: With its allure of independence and adaptability, freelancing encompasses a diverse range of fields and expertise levels. It's critical to understand the nuances of this ever-changing field before starting your freelance career. This chapter will take you on a thorough investigation, illuminating the variety of freelance employment and revealing the opportunities available to you.

2.1 *Types of Freelance Work:*

EmploymentThe world of freelancing is incredibly varied, with a wide range of positions and duties. Every industry has its own chances and problems, from programming to graphic design to content production to consulting. You may learn a lot about the demand for different skills by exploring the many kinds of freelancing. This knowledge will enable you to choose your specialization.enabling you to set yourself up for success in the cutthroat freelancing market.

2.2 Popular Freelance Platforms

Understanding the platforms that act as a bridge between independent contractors and clients is essential to navigating the freelancing market. Many platforms serve a broad spectrum of projects and businesses. We'll look at the traits and unique qualities of well-known freelance marketplaces like Upwork, Fiverr, and others in this section. You can interact with potential clients and display your skills in the best possible way by being aware of the advantages and disadvantages of each platform. As you work through this chapter, you'll gain a sophisticated perspective on the independent landscape. With this information at your disposal, you'll be more capable of navigating the variety of options that present themselves and making wise judgments that complement your goals and set of abilities.

Chapter three

Setting Up Your Freelancer Profile

In the enormous world of freelancing, your freelancer profile serves as more than simply a digital CV—rather, it is a dynamic reflection of your professional identity. In this chapter, we will take a thorough look at the components that go into creating a powerful freelancer profile. It's imperative to become an expert in profile building because it acts as your online storefront and gives prospective customers all-important first impressions.

3.1 Crafting a Compelling Bio

For clients looking for the ideal fit for their projects, your bio serves as their point of entry into your professional world. We'll get into the specifics of writing an engaging bio that not only highlights your qualifications and expertise in a clear and concise manner but also adds a little bit of your individual style. Discover powerful storytelling strategies that captivate audiences and make them want to work with you when you have a tale that speaks to the objectives of the project. Your bio becomes more than just a resume with accomplishments and talents; it tells a story about your professional experience and draws readers in. Learn how to create a distinctive and approachable profile by striking a balance between professionalism and personality.

3.2 Showcasing Your Skills and Portfolio

Your talents and portfolio serve as concrete examples of your abilities and are essential tools for persuading potential clients of your expertise. We'll look at ways to present your abilities clearly and make a lasting impression on potential employers. Discover the skill of carefully choosing samples that meet the requirements and expectations of your target market. Explore the subtleties of designing an eye-catching portfolio that not only reveals the caliber of your work but also the range of your abilities. We'll also talk about how important it is to maintain an updated portfolio that showcases your growing experience and keeps you relevant in the ever-changing freelancing market. By the time you finish this chapter, you will have gained the knowledge and understanding required to create an exceptional freelancer profile. Possessing an engaging bio and an eye-catching portfolio can help you draw in new business and create the conditions for fruitful and fulfilling partnerships.

Chapter Four

Navigating Freelance Platforms.

Freelance platforms function as vibrant marketplaces where clients and freelancers come together. The ability to navigate these digital hubs effectively is essential to realizing the full potential of your freelancing work. We take a thorough look into freelance platforms in this chapter, providing advice on how to advance your freelance business through efficient bidding techniques, project appraisal, and decision-making.

4.1 Bidding Strategies

Bidding on jobs is a sophisticated skill that can have a big impact on your career on freelance platforms; it's more than just a transaction. Explore the nuances of bidding tactics that will help you stand out from the competition and show off your special talents. We'll go into the art of creating proposals that pop, boosting your chances of landing jobs that perfectly complement.

4.2 Evaluating and Accepting Projects

Because no two projects are the same, careful project evaluation is essential to your long-term success. Discover how to strategically evaluate projects by taking into account variables including project scope, client expectations, and your own availability. We'll go into the art of judgment and provide you with a road map for accepting tasks with assurance that not only fit your skill set but also make a big impact on your career development. When evaluating a project, look for warning signs to help you avoid potential problems and ensure that any collaborations you get into will benefit both parties. During the project review phase, we will talk about how to communicate effectively with customers to lay the groundwork for open and fruitful collaborations. In this chapter, we'll explore the freelance platforms and provide you with the knowledge you need to effectively position yourself.By mastering the art of bidding and project selection, you'll not only navigate the competitive terrain effectively but also build a resilient foundation for a successful and fulfilling freelance career.

Chapter Five

Building a Strong Online Presence.

A strong online presence is essential for success in the freelance industry in the digital age. This chapter is devoted to discussing the methods and approaches that will boost your exposure and make you a reliable, in-demand freelancer. We'll go into the specifics of creating and upholding a powerful online presence, from setting up a business website to strategically using social media platforms.

5.1 Establishing a Professional Website

In the enormous world of the internet, your website is your digital storefront, a place that is exclusively yours. Discover the fundamentals of creating a polished website that represents your business identity and displays your portfolio. We'll go over the essential components of a freelancer's website, such as an interesting home page, an extensive portfolio, and a contact page that makes getting in touch with potential customers simple. Examine the advantages of owning a personal domain name and how it may affect your reputation in the workplace. Learn how to optimize your website for search engines (SEO) to make the most of your online presence and draw in relevant customers.

5.2 Leveraging Social Media for Freelance Success

Social media has developed into a vital resource for independent contractors looking to network with potential customers, exhibit their work, and keep up with market developments.

Explore practical methods for maximizing the use of social media sites like Instagram, Twitter, and LinkedIn to increase your online visibility. We'll go into the craft of creating captivating social media profiles, producing content that appeals to your target market, and cultivating deep relationships within your sector.

Learn about the potential of social media networking to establish connections that may result in worthwhile partnerships and possibilities. Learn how to create a captivating story on social media that draws clients and shows the person behind the freelancer by striking a balance between professionalism and honesty.

This chapter will give you the tools to create a digital footprint that will position you as a credible and powerful freelancer in your area while also drawing clients as you navigate the complexities of developing a strong online presence.

Chapter Six

Pricing Your Freelance Services.

Setting a price for your freelancing work is both a science and an art. This chapter delves into the complex process of figuring out how valuable you are, how to charge a price that is both lucrative and competitive, and how to create a pricing strategy that is in line with your abilities and the value you offer to clients. Determining the right pricing for your services as a freelancer starts with knowing your worth. Examine ways to measure your abilities, background, and specialties to get a fair appraisal of your professional value. We'll talk about the significance of self-awareness and how it helps you effectively convey your worth to prospective customers. Strike a careful balance between acknowledging your area of expertise and maintaining your position as a market leader. Learn how to properly present your value proposition,making it possible for you to be noticed in the congested freelance market.

6.2 Strategies for Competitive yet Profitable.

Pricing It takes skill to set pricing that is both lucrative and competitive. Explore a range of price structures, including value-based, project-based, and hourly rates. Choose the type that best suits your freelance business by learning about its benefits and drawbacks. Investigate pricing and negotiation tactics to make sure you achieve a balance between fulfilling client budgets and maintaining a successful freelance job. We'll also talk about how crucial it is to communicate your price structure in a clear and honest manner in order to build client trust and prevent misconceptions.

You will have a thorough understanding of the variables affecting your pricing decisions by the end of this chapter. Equipped with techniques to ascertain your value and establish reasonable yet competitive rates, you'll be well-positioned to confidently handle the financial facets of your freelance profession.

Chapter Seven

Effective Communication with Clients

Good communication is essential for freelancing to succeed. We'll explore the nuances of starting and continuing to communicate with clients in a clear, succinct, and professional manner in this extensive chapter. We'll look at methods to forge solid client ties and guarantee a productive working relationship, from the first contact and proposal talks to controlling client expectations during a project.

7.1 Initial Contact and Proposal Discussions

Successful freelancing collaborations frequently start with initial proposal talks and contact. Discover how to write engaging opening lines that will grab the client's interest and establish a productive working relationship. We'll talk about the skill of customizing proposals to meet the demands of certain clients, demonstrating your comprehension of their project specifications and your capacity to provide value. Examine ways to communicate effectively during the negotiating process while preserving your professional boundaries while remaining flexible.

We'll also talk about how important it is to respond to questions politely and promptly in order to build a reputation for dependability and professionalism

7.2 Managing Client Expectations

Throughout a project, maintaining client expectations requires open and honest communication. We'll explore methods for establishing deliverables, realistic project schedules, and making sure everyone is in agreement on the project's objectives.

Examine efficient methods for informing clients about any adjustments, issues, or changes in scope in order to build a cooperative and understanding partnership. Learn how to effectively handle criticism and comments so that you may use them to build stronger bonds with your clients. We'll also talk about proactive communication techniques that guarantee transparency and inspire confidence in your talents among your clients by keeping them updated on project status.

In this chapter, we'll peel back the layers of successful communication in freelancing, giving you the skills and knowledge to build and nurture long-lasting relationships with clients. Developing your communication abilities can help you stand out as a trustworthy and competent freelancer in the cutthroat industry, in addition to improving the client experience.

Chapter Eight

Delivering High-Quality Work

Chapter 8 covers the crucial stage of producing excellent work as a freelancer. This thorough investigation addresses the nuances of managing time, organizing projects, responding to modifications, and successfully incorporating customer feedback.

8.1 Time Management and Project Organization

Time management skills are critical in the world of freelancing. Discover how to prioritize your work, set reasonable deadlines, and streamline your workflow for maximum productivity. We'll explore methods and technologies that help you organize your workflow so you can fulfill deadlines without sacrificing the caliber of the products you produce.

Discover how to effectively create a project timeline that takes into account possible obstacles and permits changes. You may improve client satisfaction and your own productivity by becoming an expert in time management and project organization.

8.2 Revisions and Client Feedback Revisions are a normal aspect of working as a freelancer, and keeping clients happy requires addressing them effectively. Acquire the skill of approaching edits with a positive outlook, taking into account suggestions from clients without compromising the quality of your work. We'll talk about how to communicate effectively when discussing modifications so that everyone has a productive and enjoyable experience.

Strike a careful balance between upholding your creative vision and satisfying client expectations. Learn how to handle several iterations of modifications without jeopardizing project deadlines. Gaining proficiency in managing edits and customer feedback will help you produce work of the highest caliber and establish your reputation as a flexible and competent writer. As we navigate the terrain of producing top-notch work, this chapter provides you with the skills and knowledge required to succeed in the implementation stage of freelancing. You can meet and even surpass customer expectations by developing your time management abilities, planning your assignments efficiently, and handling modifications with grace. This will pave the way for a fruitful and long-lasting freelance business.

Chapter Nine

Handling Challenges and Setbacks

In the unpredictable world of freelancing, problems and setbacks are unavoidable. In-depth discussion of coping mechanisms is covered in Chapter 9, which covers situations including managing challenging clients, preventing freelancer burnout, and encountering unforeseen obstacles when working on projects.

9.1 Dealing with Difficult Clients.

One of the usual aspects of freelancing is working with difficult clients. Examine appropriate communication techniques for managing challenging circumstances, such as establishing limits, handling concerns in a professional manner, and resolving disputes. Discover how to take on difficult client situations as a chance for development and advancement to make sure that your freelancing career can withstand hardships.

Learn how to control client expectations and anticipate problems before they arise, laying the groundwork for more productive teamwork. Gaining resilience and proficient communication abilities will make it easier for you to turn challenging client situations into worthwhile learning opportunities.

9.2 Overcoming Freelance Burnout

In a field where boundaries are sometimes hazy, freelance burnout is a real worry. Explore methods for identifying burnout symptoms, creating a work-life balance, and putting self-care routines into place to maintain your wellbeing. We'll look at efficient time management strategies, realistic project deadlines, and integrating breaks into your work process to stave off burnout before it negatively affects your output and emotional stability.

Discuss the value of allowing for creative outlets, varying your workload, and asking mentors or other freelancers for assistance. You may create a long-lasting, satisfying freelancing career by putting self-care first and identifying the warning symptoms of burnout early on.

This chapter gives you the tools to not only overcome obstacles but also prosper in the face of misfortune as we traverse the difficulties and setbacks of freelancing. Gaining resiliency, mastering effective communication techniques, and placing your health first will set you up for long-term success in the dynamic world of freelancing.

Chapter Ten

Scaling Your Freelance Business

A thorough examination of the tactics and factors to be taken into account when growing your freelance business can be found in Chapter 10. This chapter offers advice on broadening your clientele, boosting productivity, and setting yourself up for long-term success—from hiring support to changing up your skill set.

10.1 Hiring Assistance

Your workload as a freelancer increases along with the demands on your time and energy. Examine the nuances of using help to grow your company effectively. Find out what you look for when employing support staff, subcontractors, or virtual assistants.

We'll talk about the advantages of task delegation, how to communicate assignments clearly, and how to build a cooperative working relationship that will help your freelance activities succeed overall.

Learn how to assemble a dependable team that enhances your abilities so you can concentrate on high-impact work and maintain the smooth running of your growing freelance firm.

10.2 Diversifying Your Skills and Services

An essential component of growing any firm is diversification. Investigate methods for growing your service offering and skill set to attract a larger clientele. We'll go over the advantages of learning new skills, keeping abreast of market developments, and adjusting to the changing demands of the workforce.

Find out how diversity can help your freelancing work last longer, attract a wider range of clients, and provide new opportunities. We'll go over how to add new services to your portfolio in a way that makes sense for a smooth transition and helps you stand out as a flexible freelancer in a crowded market.

By the time this chapter ends, you will have a better understanding of the life-changing process of growing your freelancing career. You will be well-equipped to handle the opportunities and challenges that come with expansion, whether by strategically employing new employees or broadening your skill set. This will pave the way for a successful and long-lasting freelance business.

Chapter Eleven

Staying Updated and Adapting to Industry Changes.

In-depth discussion of the vital component of remaining current in the ever-changing freelance industry is provided in Chapter 11. Adaptability becomes increasingly important as industries change and technologies progress. This chapter looks at ways to keep up with industry developments, modify your abilities to be competitive, and engage in ongoing professional development.

11.1 Professional Development

A successful career as a freelancer is built on lifelong learning. Investigate your options for continuing professional development, such as industry conferences, workshops, and online courses. We'll go into the advantages of learning new things, broadening your knowledge, and keeping up with new approaches and technologies.

Learn how networking with other independent contractors and business experts can promote collaboration and offer insightful information. We'll talk about the value of mentoring and asking for advice in order to overcome obstacles and take advantage of growth possibilities when working as a freelancer.

11.2 Adapting to Market Trends

The demands and expectations of clients are always evolving in the freelance industry due to market developments. Learn how to keep yourself updated about new developments in your field of expertise. In order to obtain insights into changes in customer preferences and project requirements, we'll examine the function of market research, examine industry reports, and actively participate in pertinent online forums. Discover how to modify your offerings and promotional tactics to correspond with prevailing industry patterns. Gaining insight into and capitalizing on changes in the business can help you establish yourself as a progressive independent contractor who can adapt to changing customer demands.

You will develop a deep knowledge of how crucial it is to remain current and flexible in the fast-paced world of freelancing as you work through Chapter 11. You'll not only future-proof your freelancing job by embracing networking, ongoing education, and strategic market trend adaptation, but you'll also thrive in a setting where creativity and adaptability are essential for long-term success.

Chapter Twelve

Case Studies: Successful Freelancers' Journeys

Chapter 12 takes us on an immersive and in-depth tour of the lives of successful freelancers who have forged their own pathways to success in the workplace. With a compilation of in-depth case studies covering a wide range of sectors and specializations, our goal is to provide you with a thorough grasp of the tactics, choices, and turning points that have molded these independent contractors' incredible careers.

12.1 Learning from Diverse Experiences

Put yourself in the shoes of independent contractors, whose experiences highlight the breadth and depth of the independent contractor market. These case studies provide a comprehensive understanding of the difficulties encountered and successes attained in a variety of domains, from artistic ones like writing and graphic design to technical ones like programming and consulting.

Immersing yourself in these stories will help you develop a more complex grasp of the diverse world of freelancing. Learn how independent contractors with various backgrounds overcame the early obstacles to starting their own businesses. Find out about the turning points that shaped their paths and the lessons they learned from both achievements and failures. Those looking to create their own prosperous freelancing careers can draw inspiration and useful knowledge from these real-world examples.

12.2 Uncovering Strategies for Success

Every case study has a wealth of tactics that helped these independent contractors succeed. Discover the nuances of creating enduring client connections, streamlining processes for maximum effectiveness, and maintaining your composure in the face of adversity. These success tales uncover the common threads that unite freelancers who have not only survived but thrived in the competitive freelance market.

Discover the precise strategies these independent contractors use to grow their companies, broaden their skill set, and adjust to shifting market conditions. By breaking down the tactics that made them successful, you'll gain practical knowledge that you can apply to your own freelancing work so that you may make choices that are in line with your objectives.

Through reading the accounts of these accomplished independent contractors, you will discover a plethora of motivation, useful guidance, and concrete tactics to help you carve out a successful career in the ever-changing freelance industry. This chapter's wide range of experiences acts as a road map to help you develop a successful and rewarding freelancing career.

Chapter Thirteen

Conclusion: Charting Your Freelance Journey

Chapter 13 provides a critical point of thought and action as we near the end of this extensive guide. This last chapter is devoted to assisting you in consolidating the information you have learned and offering a road map for effectively navigating your future as a freelancer.

13.1 Reflecting on Key Insights

Think back for a moment on the most important lessons learned from this tutorial. The journey has been an investigation of the many sides of freelancing, from comprehending the independent world to developing your communication skills, carefully pricing your services, and learning from the experiences of successful freelancers.

Examine how your viewpoint has changed and note the instances in which you have become more lucid. Recognize the techniques you've honed and the approaches you've taken to successfully negotiate the complex freelance industry. This introspective approach is essential to laying the groundwork for your future success and development.

13.2 Crafting Your Unique Path

Now that you're armed with information, tactics, and case studies, it's time to design your own route in the freelancing world. Realize that your path will be unique, just like your abilities and goals. Use the knowledge you've obtained to create attainable goals for yourself, such as developing your skill set, landing better-paying jobs, or growing your freelancing business.

Examine the ways in which you might adapt the tactics and knowledge gained to your own circumstances. Think about adding components of other successful freelancers' methods to your own, customizing them to fit your own goals and strengths.

13.3 Embracing Continuous Growth

The freelancing industry is dynamic, demanding flexibility and a dedication to ongoing development. Adopt a lifelong learning perspective by keeping abreast of developing trends, shifting client needs, and industry developments. Make the most of networking opportunities, professional development courses, and an open mind when it comes to honing your craft as a freelancer.

13.4 Fostering Resilience and Innovation

The path of freelancing is filled with both achievements and difficulties. Develop resilience to handle setbacks and see them as chances for growth and learning. Adopt an innovative mindset by remaining inquisitive, trying out novel strategies, and incorporating criticism to improve your processes over time.

13.5 Building a Sustainable and Fulfilling Freelance Career

To sum up, your path as a freelancer is an ongoing process that is molded by your abilities, past experiences, and the tactics you use. Keep in mind that creating a long-lasting and rewarding freelance profession is a continuous process as you map out your future.

Celebrate your successes, no matter how great or small, and seize opportunities for personal development and learning from failures. You now have the skills and information necessary to successfully navigate the complex world of freelancing, thanks to this tutorial. It's time to put these insights to use on your particular path and start a successful and rewarding freelance job. I hope your journey is characterized by ingenuity, tenacity, and unceasing development.

www.ingramcontent.com/pod-product-compliance
Lightning Source LLC
Chambersburg PA
CBHW072329270726
48658CB00016B/2232